SOPRANO & TENOR SAXOPHONE

TONS of TUNES

FOR CHURCH

AMY ADAM
MIKE HANNICKEL

T0050671

CURNOW MUSIC

Edition Number: CMP 0872.03

Amy Adam, Mike Hannickel

TONS OF TUNES for Church

Soprano & Tenor Saxophone

ISBN 90-431-1976-8

CD number: 19.047-3 CMP

CD arrangements by James L. Hosay

© Copyright 2003 by Curnow Music Press, Inc.

P.O. Box 142, Wilmore KY 40390, USA

ARRANGERS

MIKE HANNICKEL grew up in the Sacramento, California area and attended California State University, Sacramento and the University of Southern California. He has been a music teacher in Rocklin, California since 1973. He also composes and publishes exclusively with Curnow Music Press, with whom he has dozens of pieces of music in print.

AMY ADAM was raised in Grand Rapids, Minnesota and attended the University of Minnesota, Duluth graduating with a BM in band education and Flute performance. She has been a music teacher in California since 1992 and currently teaches in Rocklin, California.

TONS OF TUNES

TONS OF TUNES FOR CHURCH is filled with fun and familiar pieces that musicians love to play. All the songs have been arranged in easy keys for wind instruments. The **professional quality accompaniment CD** can be used for practice and performance. You may also choose to purchase the separately available Piano accompaniment part.

TO THE MUSIC TEACHER OR CHURCH MUSIC DIRECTOR:

TONS OF TUNES for CHURCH is a great way to help get young musicians actively involved in your church music program. Every tune in the book can be performed with the included CD accompaniment or with the separately available Piano/Organ book. All **TONS OF TUNES for CHURCH** books can be used alone or together so a variety of small ensembles can be created. Whether for prelude, offertory, church social, talent show or any other gathering, **TONS OF TUNES for CHURCH** is just what you need. Chord symbols are provided in the Piano accompaniment book for Keyboard, Guitar and combo use.

TO THE MUSICIAN:

Have **FUN** playing these songs alone or with your family and friends! Even if you have different instruments, you can still play together. Each person needs to get the **TONS OF TUNES FOR CHURCH** book for their instrument.

FOR CHURCH
CONTENTS

SOPRANO SAXOPHONE
TENOR SAXOPHONE

TONS OF TUNES FOR CHURCH

Amy Adam (ASCAP) and
Mike Hannickel (ASCAP)

1. ABIDE WITH ME

5

3. DO, LORD

4. BEAUTIFUL SAVIOR

5. FOR THE BEAUTY OF THE EARTH

6. HOLY, HOLY, HOLY

7. JESUS LOVES ME

8. MY FAITH LOOKS UP TO THEE

 0872.03 CMP • Soprano & Tenor Saxophone

9. JUST AS I AM

10. CROWN HIM WITH MANY CROWNS

11. COME, THOU ALMIGHTY KING

Moderately (♩ = 112)

12. OH, WON'T YOU SIT DOWN?

Swing (♩ = 144)

13. O FOR A THOUSAND TONGUES

14. CHILDREN OF THE HEAVENLY FATHER

15. THE CHURCH'S ONE FOUNDATION

16. NEARER MY GOD TO THEE

0872.03 CMP • Soprano & Tenor Saxophone

17. PRAISE TO THE LORD, THE ALMIGHTY

18. ALL GLORY, LAUD AND HONOR

19. ALL HAIL THE POWER

20. GOD OF GRACE AND GOD OF GLORY

21. SWING LOW, SWEET CHARIOT

22. HE'S GOT THE WHOLE WORLD IN HIS HANDS

23. GO TELL IT ON THE MOUNTAIN

24. THIS TRAIN

25. WHAT A FRIEND WE HAVE IN JESUS

26. ONWARD CHRISTIAN SOLDIERS

27. IN THE SWEET BY AND BY

28. LET US BREAK BREAD TOGETHER

29. CHRIST THE LORD IS RISEN TODAY

30. WERE YOU THERE?

31. THIS IS MY FATHER'S WORLD

32. SOFTLY AND TENDERLY JESUS IS CALLING